# COLLEGE FOOTBALL

## UNDERDOG STORIES

BY JEFF SEIDEL

UNDERDOG
SPORTS STORIES

SportsZone

An Imprint of Abdo Publishing | abdobooks.com

**abdobooks.com**

Published by Abdo Publishing, a division of ABDO, PO Box 398166, Minneapolis, Minnesota 55439.


Printed in the United States of America, North Mankato, Minnesota
092018
012019

Cover Photo: Duane Burleson/AP Images
Interior Photos: Duane Burleson/AP Images, 5, 6, 8–9, 11; Ted S. Warren/AP Images, 13, 18; Charles Krupa/AP Images, 14; Ross D. Franklin/AP Images, 17; Phil Sandlin/AP Images, 21, 25; John Raoux/AP Images, 22; Patrick Green/Cal Sport Media/AP Images, 27; Tom Sooter/Cal Sport Media/AP Images, 28; Craig Ruttle/AP Images, 30–31; Ron Schwane/AP Images, 32; Don Petersen/AP Images, 35, 36, 39; Chase Stevens/Las Vegas Review-Journal/AP Images, 41, 42, 45

Editor: Patrick Donnelly
Series Designer: Melissa Martin

**Library of Congress Control Number: 2018949193**

**Publisher's Cataloging-in-Publication Data**

Names: Seidel, Jeff, author.
Title: College football underdog stories / by Jeff Seidel.
Description: Minneapolis, Minnesota : Abdo Publishing, 2019 | Series: Underdog sports stories | Includes online resources and index.
Identifiers: ISBN 9781532117619 (lib. bdg.) | ISBN 9781532170478 (ebook)
Subjects: LCSH: American football--Juvenile literature. | College athletes--Juvenile literature. | Upsets in sports--Juvenile literature. | Winning and losing--Juvenile literature.
Classification: DDC 796.332630--dc23

# TABLE OF CONTENTS

CHAPTER 1

# A MOUNTAIN-SIZED UPSET

People love to cheer for the underdog in sports. Whether it's a team that seems to have the odds stacked against it or a player who comes out of nowhere to become a star, college football provides plenty of chances for underdogs to pull off a surprise.

Appalachian State is a perfect example. The small college located in Boone, North Carolina, had developed a decent football program by 2007. But the Mountaineers played in the Football Championship Subdivision (FCS),

**Michigan running back Mike Hart (20) didn't have much room to run against the Mountaineers.**

which used to be called Division I-AA. Its members are smaller schools with fewer resources. The top high school players in the country usually move on to play for Football Bowl Subdivision (FBS) programs, the top level of Division I football.

**Quarterback Armanti Edwards came up big all day long for the Mountaineers.**

Michigan is an FBS power and has been one of the top teams in college football for decades. The Wolverines play in the biggest stadium in the country. "The Big House," as it's known, seats more than 107,000 roaring Michigan fans, giving the Wolverines a home-field advantage like few others in the nation.

## THREE-TIME CHAMPIONS

The Mountaineers went on to post a 13–2 record in 2007, and they won their third straight national title with a 49–21 victory over Delaware and future Super Bowl Most Valuable Player (MVP) Joe Flacco. Meanwhile, Michigan went 9–4 and won the Capital One Bowl over Heisman Trophy winner Tim Tebow and Florida.

An FCS team doesn't often get a chance to play in an environment like that. Michigan set up a game with the Mountaineers to start the 2007 season, offering

Appalachian State $400,000 to come to its big stadium for the season opener.

The Mountaineers were no typical FCS pushover. Appalachian State won consecutive FCS national championships in 2005 and 2006. Quarterback Armanti Edwards passed for 2,251 yards and ran for 1,153 more as a freshman in 2006.

But this was Michigan. The Wolverines were consistently strong, often dominant. They'd spent at least one week in the national top 10 every season since 1968, and head coach Lloyd Carr led them to the national championship

**Appalachian State running back Kevin Richardson tries to quiet the crowd at the Big House.**

in 1997. In 2007 Michigan was ranked fifth in the season's first national poll. Even as good as Appalachian State was, this looked like a mismatch.

However, the Mountaineers were ready. They scored three consecutive touchdowns in the second quarter, two on passes from Edwards and the other on his 6-yard run en route to a 28–17 halftime lead.

The second half was all Michigan. After the teams traded field goals, Wolverines running back Mike Hart scored on a short touchdown run late in the third quarter.

Then, with less than five minutes to play, Hart broke off a 54-yard touchdown run to put Michigan on top 32–31.

When Michigan's Brandent Englemon intercepted Edwards on the first play of the next drive, it looked like the dream had died for Appalachian State. But the Mountaineers' defense held and their special teams came through, blocking Jason Gingell's 43-yard field goal attempt. The Mountaineers took over on their own 26-yard line with 1:37 to play.

Then it was Edwards's time to shine. He ran for 18 yards on the first play. Then he completed four straight passes for a total of 55 yards. With 26 seconds left, Julian Rauch made a 24-yard field goal and the Mountaineers were back on top 34–32.

But Michigan wasn't done. From his own 34-yard line with 15 seconds to play, quarterback Chad Henne heaved a long pass down the right sideline. Wide receiver Mario Manningham got behind the defense and hauled it in at the Appalachian State 20-yard line. If Gingell could split the uprights on a 37-yard field goal attempt, the Wolverines would dodge the bullet.

But the Michigan kicker never got a chance. The ball had barely left his foot when it was smothered by safety Corey Lynch, who had burst through the Michigan line.

**Jason Gingell grimaces as the ball bounces past him after Corey Lynch blocked his attempted game-winning field goal.**

Lynch scooped up the blocked kick and rumbled down the field as the clock ran out. Gingell chased him down before he reached the end zone, but it didn't matter. Appalachian State had pulled off the monumental upset.

# TRICKS TRIP SOONERS

Chris Petersen had a bunch of trick plays in his pocket, and the Boise State coach had a knack for picking the perfect time to call them. He knew he'd need to rely on some misdirection and sleight of hand if his Broncos were going to have a chance against the Oklahoma Sooners in the 2007 Fiesta Bowl.

The seventh-ranked Sooners were led by future National Football League (NFL) star Adrian Peterson, as fast and strong a running back as the college game

The Broncos had their hands full with Adrian Peterson (28) all day.

had seen in years. Senior quarterback Paul Thompson was a 60 percent passer who threw for 22 touchdowns on the season. Oklahoma was riding an eight-game winning streak, had an 11–2 record, and won the Big 12 Conference title.

The Broncos were on a roll, too. In Chris Petersen's first year as head coach, they had finished the regular season 12–0 and ranked No. 9 in the nation. But the Western Athletic Conference didn't provide the same level of competition that the Sooners faced in the Big 12. Even though Oklahoma was favored by just seven points, many observers did

**Marty Tadman rejoices after his interception return gave the Broncos a big third-quarter lead.**

not expect a close game. *Sports Illustrated* later said that it "was supposed to be a romp."

However, someone forgot to tell that to Boise State. The Broncos took charge early, with the senior duo of quarterback Jared Zabransky and receiver Drisan James hooking up for two long touchdowns in the first half. When safety Marty Tadman returned an interception 27 yards for a touchdown midway through the third quarter, Boise State led 28–10.

But Oklahoma roared back. Adrian Peterson scored on an 8-yard run. Garrett Hartley made a field goal. Thompson threw a touchdown pass, and a two-point conversion tied the game 28–28 with less than a minute and a half to play.

Then the Broncos appeared to give the game away. Sooners cornerback Marcus Walker picked off a Zabransky pass and brought it back 33 yards for a touchdown. With 1:02 left in the game, Oklahoma led 35–28.

But Boise State would not give up. The Broncos reached midfield and were faced with fourth-and-18 with 18 seconds left. That's when Chris Petersen reached into his bag of tricks for the first time.

Zabransky hit James over the middle 15 yards downfield. James then flipped a lateral to teammate Jerard Rabb, who was racing across the field from the opposite direction. Rabb took off down the left sideline and sprinted to the end zone. The play—known as a hook-and-lateral—worked to perfection. The extra-point kick tied the game 35–35, forcing overtime.

As thrilled as the Broncos were to get a second chance, 60 minutes of being pushed around by Oklahoma's massive offensive line had taken a toll on the defense. The Sooners started with the ball in overtime, but they didn't have it long. On the first play, Adrian Peterson steamrolled

Boise State's Jerard Rabb (1) dives into the end zone with his game-saving touchdown at the end of the fourth quarter.

the Broncos' defense for a 25-yard touchdown run. Hartley's extra-point kick made it 42–35.

Boise State needed a touchdown to stay alive. Its drive reached the 5-yard line, where it was fourth down. Then it was time for trick play number two. As the offense lined up, Zabransky sprinted to the far-left side of the field. Wide receiver Vinny Perretta took the snap, rolled to his right, and threw a touchdown pass to tight end Derek Schouman. That made the score 42–41.

**Ian Johnson, *left*, takes a behind-the-back handoff from Jared Zabransky (5) on the Broncos' final trick play of the night.**

Time to kick the game-tying extra point, right? Wrong. Perhaps sensing that his defense was out of gas, Chris Petersen decided to go for the two-point conversion and the win. And that meant it was time for one last trick play.

## POM-POM PROPOSAL

Ian Johnson added to the fun after the game-winning play. With the TV cameras rolling, he dropped to one knee and proposed to his girlfriend, Boise State cheerleader Chrissy Popadics. She said yes.

Zabransky took the snap and wound up as if he was going to pass to one of three receivers on the right. But his right hand was empty. The ball was in his left hand, which he tucked behind his back. Tailback Ian Johnson grabbed the ball and ran untouched into the end zone, completing one of the most memorable upsets in Fiesta Bowl history.

# TRIPLE THE PLEASURE

The Georgia Southern Eagles traveled to Gainesville, Florida, to play the slumping Florida Gators late in the 2013 season. Even though Florida had lost five straight games, the Gators were a 28-point favorite heading into this contest.

After all, Georgia Southern was an FCS team, while the Gators were one of the big dogs in the Southeastern Conference (SEC). The smaller schools rarely beat FBS teams, especially those with SEC pedigrees.

**Georgia Southern quarterback Kevin Ellison had a big day against Florida.**

But Florida's coaching staff was concerned about the style of offense that the Eagles ran. Georgia Southern used a run-heavy scheme called the triple option. It used to be extremely popular before passing became more common in football starting in the 1940s. These days, Army, Navy, and Georgia Tech run it with success, but it's not seen nearly as much as it once was.

**Florida head coach Will Muschamp didn't like what he saw as the Eagles ran circles around his defense.**

Still, the Gators never had lost to an FCS team and had outscored their previous seven FCS opponents by an average of 45 points. So when Florida jumped out to a 10–0 lead in the second quarter, it looked like the game would go according to plan.

Not so fast. The triple option started clicking and Georgia Southern began chewing up big chunks of yardage on the ground. The Eagles ended up averaging almost 8 yards per play on the day.

## TRIPLE HEADACHES

The concept behind the triple option is pretty simple, even if the offense can be difficult to defend. The quarterback takes the snap and does one of three things. Depending on what he sees from the defense, he can keep the ball, hand it off to the fullback plowing straight into the line, or pitch to a running back out wide. Many teams put three running backs in the backfield with the quarterback to help confuse the defense.

Jerick McKinnon ran for 125 yards on nine carries. Kevin Ellison rushed 15 times for 118 more yards. And William Banks added 94 yards on 11 carries as the Gators just could not slow the running game.

Ellison scored two touchdowns and Banks added another with 32 seconds left in the third quarter to give Georgia Southern a 20–10 lead. Florida fought back with 10 straight points, including a 46-yard touchdown pass from Skyler Mornhinweg to Solomon Patton to tie the game with 5:41 to play.

But the Eagles marched right back down the field, covering 75 yards on just five plays, all on the ground. McKinnon scored the game-winning touchdown, taking a quick pitch and getting around the right end easily to score the touchdown, which gave the Eagles a 26–20 lead with 2:57 to play.

Florida tried to fight back, reaching the Georgia Southern 17-yard line in the final seconds. Mornhinweg

**Georgia Southern wide receiver Allen Lee celebrates with fans after the Eagles pulled off the upset.**

took two shots at the end zone, both falling incomplete, and it was over. Georgia Southern 26, Florida 20.

It was a fitting end for the Gators, who had already lost 10 players to season-ending injuries, a big reason they finished the season losing seven straight games. To make things worse for Florida, it lost to a team that did not complete one pass in the game. The Eagles finished the game 0-for-3 through the air but rushed for 429 yards and pulled off an amazing upset in the process.

# CHAPTER 4

# LONG ROAD TO STARDOM

Baker Mayfield grew up in Texas, which means he grew up playing football. But even though he quarterbacked Lake Travis High School to a state title in 2011 during his junior year, he wasn't highly recruited. In fact, Mayfield only received scholarship offers from three schools—Florida Atlantic, New Mexico, and Rice.

Instead, Mayfield decided to attend Texas Tech as a walk-on, meaning he did not receive a scholarship like

Baker Mayfield won the starting quarterback job as a true freshman walk-on at Texas Tech.

TEXAS TECH
6

many players do. Instead, he paid his own way to college. Usually walk-on players don't see much action, especially freshmen walk-ons. But starting quarterback Michael Brewer got hurt before the season started. Mayfield beat out the rest of the competition and won the starting job to start the 2013 season.

Mayfield transferred to Oklahoma, where he became a star.

Texas Tech is known for its pass-happy offense, and Mayfield took full advantage of the opportunity to fill the air with footballs. In his first start he completed an eye-popping 43 of 60 passes for 413 yards and four touchdowns against Southern Methodist University. Through five weeks, Texas Tech was 5–0 and Mayfield had completed almost two-thirds of his passing attempts for nearly 300 yards per game.

But an injury sidelined Mayfield for a month, and he did not play as well when he returned. He threw as many touchdown passes as interceptions and Tech lost all three games he started in November. When he found out he'd have to compete for the starting job again the next summer, he decided to transfer to Oklahoma. After sitting out a year due to transfer rules, Mayfield won the starting job in 2015 and put together quite a run, despite concerns about his size.

Mayfield is listed as 6 feet even or sometimes at 6 feet 1 (185 cm). But many suspect he's actually a bit shorter. Bigger schools and NFL teams like tall quarterbacks, but Mayfield showed his talent at Oklahoma.

During his three years there, Mayfield grew into one of the nation's best quarterbacks. In 40 starts he threw 119 touchdown passes and only 21 interceptions and averaged just over 300 yards per game. The Sooners lost only six games in three seasons with Mayfield at the helm.

## THIRD TIME'S THE CHARM

Baker Mayfield came close twice before winning the Heisman Trophy as a senior. He finished fourth in the Heisman Trophy voting in 2015 and third in 2016. He became just the fifth player with three top-four finishes in the history of the award.

Everything came together in the 2017 season, when the senior had his best year ever. Mayfield completed 285 of 404 passes for 4,627 yards.

In addition, he threw 43 touchdown passes and was intercepted only six times en route to winning the Heisman Trophy as the nation's top college football player.

The quarterback also played a big role in the Sooners winning a third straight Big 12 title. They also made it to the College Football Playoffs, where they lost to Georgia 54–48 in double overtime at the Rose Bowl. Mayfield threw for 287 yards and two touchdowns and even caught a 2-yard touchdown pass that day. That loss kept the Sooners from reaching the

**Mayfield brought home the Heisman Trophy after his senior season.**

**The Cleveland Browns put their faith in Mayfield.**

national championship game against Alabama, but it was still a memorable run.

After that came the question of where Mayfield would be picked in the 2018 NFL Draft. The concerns about his size were accompanied by questions about his brash personality that rubbed people the wrong way at times. But the Cleveland Browns looked past all of that and made him the No. 1 overall pick. That decision was a bit of a surprise, because the Browns were trying to rebuild their franchise and needed a quarterback who could shoulder that burden. But they also acquired veteran Tyrod Taylor with the intention of giving Mayfield time to learn the ropes.

It turned out Mayfield's debut came earlier than expected. He took over for Taylor late in the second quarter of a Week 3 home game against the New York Jets. Mayfield went on to complete 17 of 23 passes for 201 yards and led the Browns back from a 14–0 deficit to a 21–17 victory, their first since the 2016 season.

Turning the Browns into winners is a tall order. But if anyone can do it, it's a guy who went from walk-on to transfer to Heisman Trophy-winner to the NFL's No. 1 draft pick. Baker Mayfield had come a long way in a short time.

CHAPTER 5

# HOKIE HEADACHE

The Virginia Tech Hokies came into the second week of the 2010 football season looking to bounce back from a tough loss in their season opener against third-ranked Boise State. Next up were the James Madison University (JMU) Dukes, an FCS team from upstate Virginia. The Hokies had not lost to an FCS team since 1985, and they'd outscored James Madison 90–0 in their previous two meetings.

Antoine Hopkins (56) and Virginia Tech kept the James Madison offense under wraps early.

JMU
MADISON
9
HOKIES
56

James Madison had one of the more successful FCS programs, but Virginia Tech and its strong offense were expected to take care of business. The No. 13 Hokies rolled into the game as 32.5-point favorites.

The Hokies moved the ball well most of the game. They ran for 238 yards, including 86 from quarterback Tyrod Taylor. However, they struggled to turn that yardage into points. After a first-quarter touchdown pass by Taylor, Virginia Tech drove inside the JMU 25-yard line three

**Drew Dudzik (9) scores one of his two rushing touchdowns in the second half as the Dukes roared back to take the lead.**

more times, but each time the Hokies had to settle for a field goal.

Virginia Tech also showed signs of sloppiness that hinted at big trouble. Early in the second quarter, Taylor lost a fumble in Dukes territory. Then JMU running back Jamal Sullivan took a short pass 77 yards to the end zone, breaking numerous tackles along the way. Poor tackling, untimely penalties, and three turnovers ended up proving costly to the Hokies.

Chris Hazley's third field goal gave Virginia Tech a 16–7 lead early in the third quarter. But that's when the Dukes began to move the ball. They went on a 15-play, 66-yard drive capped by Drew Dudzik's 7-yard touchdown run. That cut the lead to 16–14.

Three plays later, James Madison got the ball back when Jonathan Williams intercepted a Taylor pass at his own 29-yard line. The Dukes marched down the field again, with Dudzik running it in from 12 yards out. James Madison had a 21–16 lead with 13:45 remaining.

The Hokies tried to fight back, and they certainly had their chances. They drove inside the JMU 20-yard line, but defensive back Leavander Jones knocked away Taylor's pass to Jarrett Boykin in the end zone on fourth down. After forcing a James Madison punt, the Hokies again took it deep inside JMU territory, looking for the go-ahead touchdown. But running back Darren Evans fumbled at the 10-yard line and the Dukes took over again with 5:21 to play.

James Madison didn't give Virginia Tech another chance. The Dukes chewed up ground and ran down the clock. They were

## A RARE FEAT

The Hokies, who went on to win their next 11 games and play in the Orange Bowl, were the second ranked FBS team to lose to an FCS squad. The first, of course, was Michigan, which was ranked No. 5 in the nation when it lost to Appalachian State in 2007.

Leavander Jones, *left*, makes a big play to break up a pass intended for the Hokies' Jarrett Boykin in the fourth quarter.

about to punt the ball back with 13 seconds left, but the Hokies committed a penalty that gave the Dukes a first down. That was it—game over.

Dudzik helped the JMU cause by completing 5 of 8 passes for 121 yards, including three that gave the Dukes big first downs in the second half. Coupled with errors by the mistake-prone Hokies, it was just enough to pull off a major upset.

CHAPTER 6

# MISSION POSSIBLE

The Howard University Bison weren't thought to be much of a threat when they faced the University of Nevada-Las Vegas (UNLV) Rebels in the 2017 season opener. UNLV was favored by a whopping 45 points. That means the Rebels were expected to win by at least six touchdowns and extra points plus a field goal.

It was a rare position for UNLV to be favored, especially by that many points. The Rebels were coming off a 4–8 season and had finished with a winning record just once

**Howard head coach Mike London gives his players vocal encouragement during their 2017 game at UNLV.**

since 2000. However, in a similar spot a year before, UNLV had drilled FCS foe Jackson State 63–13. Surely it could handle the Bison without much trouble.

Howard understood it was a big underdog. The Bison had won a total of three games in the past two seasons and were starting with a new coach. Mike London had taken over the team after working as an assistant coach at nearby University of Maryland. He also had been a head coach at the University of Virginia.

**Howard defensive back Travon Hunt, *right*, wraps up UNLV wide receiver Devonte Boyd.**

London wanted to change the way players thought about the program. He tried to inspire them by using the phrase "Mission Possible"—a play on words regarding the "Mission Impossible" movies—as the team slogan for the 2017 season.

To make that mission possible, Howard turned to a freshman quarterback named Caylin Newton. He's the younger brother of former Heisman winner Cam Newton, who also led the Carolina Panthers to the Super Bowl. The younger Newton lived up to his pedigree against UNLV. He ran for 190 yards and two touchdowns and threw for 140 yards and another score. And his biggest plays came late in the see-saw battle, when his team needed him the most.

Howard jumped out to a 21–9 lead before UNLV scored 24 straight points. That gave the Rebels a 33–21 lead with 6:45 left in the third quarter. Howard fought back with two running touchdowns from Anthony Philyaw to retake the

## OH, BROTHER

Caylin Newton went on to show that his performance against UNLV was no fluke. The Bison finished 6–2 in the Mid-Eastern Athletic Conference (MEAC), and Newton was named the MEAC Freshman of the Year. He also was the first freshman in conference history to surpass 3,000 total yards in a season as he ran for 753 yards and passed for 2,432 more.

lead 36–33 early in the fourth quarter. But UNLV drove back down the field and scored on a short touchdown run to go back up 40–36.

Then it was Newton's time to shine as he converted two third-and-6 plays to set up another scoring opportunity. First he scrambled for 14 yards to keep the drive going at midfield. Three plays later, he threw a 42-yard pass to Philyaw that put the Bison deep in UNLV territory. Finally, Newton scored on a 4-yard run. The extra point gave Howard a 43–40 lead with 7:34 remaining, and the Bison held on for the win.

The 43–40 victory was Howard's first against an FBS opponent. A year earlier, Maryland routed Howard 52–13 in the season opener. But this was a new era in Howard football. London and Newton led the Bison to a 7–4 overall record, and they proved that beating a 45-point favorite was not an impossible mission after all.

Bison players celebrate their victory on the sideline.

# GLOSSARY

**cornerback**

A defensive player who normally covers wide receivers.

**end zone**

The end of the field where teams try to score touchdowns.

**extra point**

A kick worth one point attempted after a touchdown.

**fullback**

An offensive player who sometimes runs with the football but is also responsible for blocking.

**lateral**

A pass that goes sideways or backward.

**poll**

A survey of opinions on a subject, often used to rank college football teams during the season.

**scholarship**

Money awarded to a student to pay for education expenses.

**snap**

The start of each play, when the center hikes the ball between his legs to a player behind him, usually the quarterback.

**transfer**

To move to a new school.

# MORE INFORMATION

## BOOKS


Mason, Tyler. *Football Trivia*. Minneapolis, MN: Abdo Publishing, 2016.

Rule, Heather. *Sports' Greatest Turnarounds*. Minneapolis, MN: Abdo Publishing, 2018.

Wilner, Barry. *Total Football*. Minneapolis, MN: Abdo Publishing, 2017.


# ONLINE RESOURCES

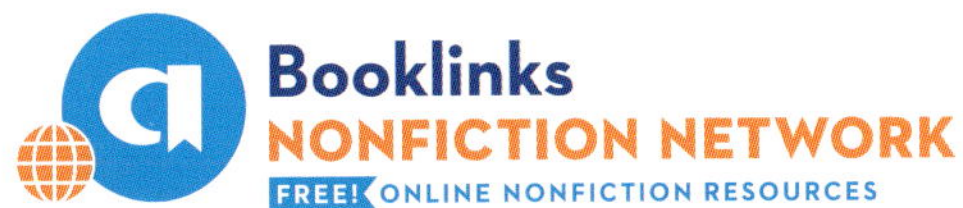


To learn more about college football underdogs, visit abdobooklinks.com. These links are routinely monitored and updated to provide the most current information available.

# INDEX



# ABOUT THE AUTHOR

Jeff Seidel lives in Baltimore with his wife, two kids, and two cats. He has written several books on many sports over the last 15 years.